Affirm Your Affirmations

in 21 Days

DR. STACI SNAIR

Edited by Lil Barcaski & Katy Faith Snair

Published by: GWN Publishing
www.GWNPublishing.com

Cover Design: Kristina Conatser

ISBN: 978-1-959608-58-5

For more information about bulk purchase discounts or bringing Staci to a live event, please contact Dr. Staci Snair info@drstacisnair.com

I dedicate this book to Ethan William. From the moment you were born I knew there was something magical about you. Such an old soul, so gentle and so loving. Although you graced this earth for only a few short years, your wisdom and Love continue to guide me each and every day. My Love and Gratitude for you are eternal.

PREFACE

There is so much talk about manifestation, affirmations, and gratitude, yet does anyone really know how or where to begin applying this to their own lives? Admittedly, I struggled with coming up with the right phrase, or what to even ask for. Hence, my motivation for writing this resource book for you.

This is meant to be a guide, not a pass/fail college class. Yes, commit yourself to the process, but do not agonize over the details of each task. My hope is that you enjoy the process, experience a welcome shift in your life, and choose to go through the process again and again with the knowledge that you are capable of creating the life you truly desire.

A note about mediation:

It is important to remember, meditation is meant to be an opportunity for growth and healing. Trust me when I say, even those that are experienced with meditation will still have some days where they might struggle with quieting their mind. The key here is to continue the practice without any judgment of yourself. Remember every experience is an opportunity to have Grace with yourself as you open your mind and heart to the possibilities that await you.

Are you ready to change your life?

Here
we
GO!

DAY *1*

Congratulations! You have taken the first step in making a positive and lasting change in your life. Deciding you want to make a shift is perhaps the most difficult part of this process. Take a moment and acknowledge this conscious choice you have made. Feel excited and proud; you deserve a pat on the back for taking charge of your life.

Soak it in.

Now, let's get started on your first action step. Brainstorm the different shifts or changes that you would like to have in your life. This is going to be a laundry list of sorts. It is important to understand that just because we want to grow as a person, and make improvements in our life, does NOT mean there is anything wrong with us. I would be more concerned about you if you stated your life is perfect and there is nothing to improve upon in any area.

Make your rambling list today, then put it to the side. Tomorrow I will guide you through what you will do next with your list.

＿＿＿＿＿＿＿＿＿＿＿＿＿＿＿＿＿＿＿＿＿＿＿＿＿＿＿＿＿＿＿＿＿＿

＿＿＿＿＿＿＿＿＿＿＿＿＿＿＿＿＿＿＿＿＿＿＿＿＿＿＿＿＿＿＿＿＿＿

＿＿＿＿＿＿＿＿＿＿＿＿＿＿＿＿＿＿＿＿＿＿＿＿＿＿＿＿＿＿＿＿＿＿

＿＿＿＿＿＿＿＿＿＿＿＿＿＿＿＿＿＿＿＿＿＿＿＿＿＿＿＿＿＿＿＿＿＿

＿＿＿＿＿＿＿＿＿＿＿＿＿＿＿＿＿＿＿＿＿＿＿＿＿＿＿＿＿＿＿＿＿＿

＿＿＿＿＿＿＿＿＿＿＿＿＿＿＿＿＿＿＿＿＿＿＿＿＿＿＿＿＿＿＿＿＿＿

＿＿＿＿＿＿＿＿＿＿＿＿＿＿＿＿＿＿＿＿＿＿＿＿＿＿＿＿＿＿＿＿＿＿

＿＿＿＿＿＿＿＿＿＿＿＿＿＿＿＿＿＿＿＿＿＿＿＿＿＿＿＿＿＿＿＿＿＿

＿＿＿＿＿＿＿＿＿＿＿＿＿＿＿＿＿＿＿＿＿＿＿＿＿＿＿＿＿＿＿＿＿＿

＿＿＿＿＿＿＿＿＿＿＿＿＿＿＿＿＿＿＿＿＿＿＿＿＿＿＿＿＿＿＿＿＿＿

＿＿＿＿＿＿＿＿＿＿＿＿＿＿＿＿＿＿＿＿＿＿＿＿＿＿＿＿＿＿＿＿＿＿

＿＿＿＿＿＿＿＿＿＿＿＿＿＿＿＿＿＿＿＿＿＿＿＿＿＿＿＿＿＿＿＿＿＿

＿＿＿＿＿＿＿＿＿＿＿＿＿＿＿＿＿＿＿＿＿＿＿＿＿＿＿＿＿＿＿＿＿＿

＿＿＿＿＿＿＿＿＿＿＿＿＿＿＿＿＿＿＿＿＿＿＿＿＿＿＿＿＿＿＿＿＿＿

＿＿＿＿＿＿＿＿＿＿＿＿＿＿＿＿＿＿＿＿＿＿＿＿＿＿＿＿＿＿＿＿＿＿

＿＿＿＿＿＿＿＿＿＿＿＿＿＿＿＿＿＿＿＿＿＿＿＿＿＿＿＿＿＿＿＿＿＿

＿＿＿＿＿＿＿＿＿＿＿＿＿＿＿＿＿＿＿＿＿＿＿＿＿＿＿＿＿＿＿＿＿＿

＿＿＿＿＿＿＿＿＿＿＿＿＿＿＿＿＿＿＿＿＿＿＿＿＿＿＿＿＿＿＿＿＿＿

＿＿＿＿＿＿＿＿＿＿＿＿＿＿＿＿＿＿＿＿＿＿＿＿＿＿＿＿＿＿＿＿＿＿

Your only other action step today is to meditate. I will give you my suggestion, for meditation each day, however, like this whole program . . .

THE CHOICE, IN EVERY MOMENT, IS YOURS.

At the beginning of this 21 Day shift, it is not uncommon to have a lot of thoughts and self judgments circling around in your mind. It is for this reason I am suggesting you do a meditation that is designed to simply quiet your mind. I have found the most effective way to do this is using counting breaths.

» *As you breathe in through your nose, slowly count: 1, 2, 3, 4.*

» *Next, hold your breath for half this count. . . so 1, 2.*

» *Then, slowly exhale through your mouth to the same count as you inhaled, 1, 2, 3, 4.*

» *Repeat until you feel calm and your mind is quiet, or at least a little calmer and quieter. You can either let this happen in its natural time, or you may choose to designate an allotted period of time that you want to meditate for. This can be anywhere from 2 to 20+ minutes.*

You are looking for quality versus quantity. Meaning, it is a more effective meditation to achieve a peaceful state for two minutes, then to struggle for 20 minutes. If your mind wanders once or twice in a meditation, and you can gently bring yourself back to focus, that is great. However, if you are meeting with resistance and frustration when your mind wanders, continuing to sit and struggle is counter-productive. Take a break and try again, either later in the day or even the next day. Remember to have patience and understanding for yourself that you are learning a new skill.

As an alternative to the meditation described above, you are welcome to use my general meditation that is posted on my website. http://www.drstacisnair.com

There are many, many different meditations out there. You are free to use any of them here. My recommendation is you stick with one that feels good and allow yourself to build a relationship with a single meditation. After you have built up your meditation muscle, you may choose to switch up your meditations. However, for this process, I strongly recommend the meditations I have given to you.

DAY *2*

Awesome, you are back! Take a deep breath, and allow the stress to release with your exhale. Remind yourself that this is a process. It takes some time to get things rolling, but you are ready and YOU ARE SO WORTH THE EFFORT!

Today you are going to look at that laundry list of shifts and changes. If yours is really long, you might want to go get a couple of different color highlighters, pens or colored pencils.

Go ahead, I will be right here.

The brain likes to look at things in a more organized manner. Therefore, take a look at your list from yesterday. Are there any items that are similar in nature? Typically, when we make a rambling list, which is what was suggested of you, items on the list become redundant. Highlight similar subjects in one color. There is no limit right now to the subject areas on your list. Take a deep breath, embrace your inner child, and go color!

Great job! Now this next part might be a little challenging. From these groupings, narrow down your list to three changes, or subjects, where you want to make shifts or changes. Take your time in making your choices. Look for the subjects that bring you peace, excitement, hope, etc. Stay away from the subjects that bring fear or dread.

The goal is to make shifts/changes in specific areas of your life, but note that a general, overall shift will also be created. Therefore you might not be targeting the "fear or dread," but you will have a positive effect on them. So, take a nice centering breath, and consider your choices.

After you are done, pat yourself on the back. I think Day 2 contains a very challenging task, and you did it! Now, pencils down class.

Your reward is your meditation. Although you might not be truly enjoying meditation yet, I promise that with some practice, an open mind and heart, these will absolutely grow on you.

As I stated yesterday, the meditation you do is always your choice. Here is the one I had recommended yesterday.

» *Breathe in through your nose as you slowly count 1, 2, 3, 4.*

» *Hold your breath for 1, 2.*

» *Then, slowly exhale through your mouth 1, 2, 3, 4.*

» *Repeat until you feel at least a little calmer and your mind is a little quieter, or until your designated meditation time has been achieved.*

Keep in mind, you can practice this breathing technique throughout your day too. Although it is a wonderful meditation tool, it can also be used to calm yourself in any situation. Taking even just one or two counting breaths can help lessen anxiety and diffuse frustration and anger. The benefits are endless!

DAY *3*

Time to dig a little deeper. Take your three shifts/changes and write a descriptive account of how your life would be different with each of these shifts/changes. Please write these as three separate accounts totally independent of one another.

Remember this is not an English term paper. Spelling and grammar do not carry any credence here. Instead, be vulnerable, be honest, be authentically you. Yeah, go ahead and ramble a bit too, it tends to get those feelings flowing. Just keep the pen moving.

Take a deep breath, tap into your feelings, and get raw.

You can choose to do the breathing meditation here. It can be very helpful in getting started especially if you are feeling unsure where to start or are overwhelmed with thoughts.

» *Breathe in through your nose as you slowly count 1, 2, 3, 4.*

» *Hold your breath for 1, 2.*

» *Then, slowly exhale through your mouth 1, 2, 3, 4.*

» *Repeat until you feel at least a little calmer and your mind is a little quieter, or until your designated meditation time has been achieved.*

1

#2

#3

Woo Hoo! You are well on your way to making shifts/changes. Do not underestimate how much work these last few exercises took to accomplish. It is more than time you are putting in. You are putting your effort, your emotions, and your belief into yourself. . . these are invaluable.

Pause for a moment and give yourself due credit for all that you are investing in yourself.

YOU ARE WORTH IT!

And now, let's meditate. Even if you chose to do it before your writing, I would recommend doing it again now. Writing can stir up feelings, most likely ones we are trying to work through and release. Meditating after stirring these feelings up will help settle and center yourself again. I highly recommend it.

Here is the one I have been recommending. This is a foundational exercise that we will be building upon throughout the 21 days.

And. . .

» *Breathe in through your nose as you slowly count 1, 2, 3, 4.*

» *Hold your breath for 1, 2.*

» *Then, slowly exhale through your mouth 1, 2, 3, 4.*

» *Repeat until you feel at least a little calmer and your mind is a little quieter. Or, until your designated meditation time has been achieved.*

If you are setting a timer, and the time is on the shorter side, maybe 3 - 5 minutes, consider adding 20 - 30 seconds every few days. Remember, meditation is a muscle building exercise.

DAY 4

Time for reflection. Take a look at your descriptive account regarding your shifts/changes from yesterday. Do you notice any sequence or theme to these ideas? Or maybe a root feeling, or cause to why you may want these shifts/changes? You may or may not. Either is okay. Really! There is no correct or A+ answer to any of these questions. Our personal life experiences are the perfect lens in which we see our lessons at any given time.

Yesterday, I suggested that you meditate before you began to write. Today, I am going to instruct you to mediate before you write your reflection. Often, when we begin to build our meditation muscle, our mind can clear enough to gain a new, or deeper perspective when we look at a situation after meditating. I know you may only be on your fourth day of meditation ever, but let's give it a whirl. Remember, no judgment! We are simply testing the waters and seeing if any shifts are starting to occur.

Ready?

» *Breathe in through your nose as you slowly count 1, 2, 3, 4.*

» *Hold your breath for 1, 2.*

» *Then, slowly exhale through your mouth 1, 2, 3, 4.*

» *Repeat until you feel a little calmer and your mind is quieter, or the designated period of time that you chose to meditate for has ended.*

Now, take another look at the descriptive account of your shifts/changes from yesterday. Write down any reactions that might come up for you as you reread them. These can be emotional, or physical. Do you recognize any similar themes, or complete contrasts? You can also write down anything that you feel called to make a note of. Remember, this is about you and for you. You've got this!

DAY 5

Over the last two days, you have spent a good deal of time thinking and feeling through the three shifts/changes you are considering in your life. Today, you are going to rank them in the order you feel would be best for you. You will only be working on one shift/change in this 21 day process. Please understand, although we are only focusing on one shift/ change, this doesn't mean others won't organically occur. They may. After this round, you may decide to work on shift/change number 2 next month, or you might totally change directions. But, don't think or wonder about that right now. It is best to simply focus on the specific shift/change you would like to make through this round of the process.

There are two directions of thought when choosing your shift/change. The first is to make your choice based on the ease you will have in making the shift. This is by no means a cop out. Instead, the theory of this choice is based on momentum. What I mean is, as we begin to successfully make shifts/changes in our lives, it subsequently becomes easier for more challenging shifts to occur.

The second direction is making a shift or change in the areas where it will most likely make the greatest impact. These tend to have us meeting with more resistance which could lead to increased frustration and discouragement in believing in oneself and this process. In my experience, the first choice is the best for not only completing this process, but for making lasting shifts/changes in your life and increasing your self-esteem. It carries the likelihood for you to continue making positive shifts/changes in your life going forward.

With this in mind, rank your choices.

Did you choose your number 1?

Great!

Now sit in a comfortable and quiet spot as you prepare to meditate. Taking the time to meditate before you begin writing will assist you in limiting self-judgment, as well as help you to think and feel more clearly. This is essential at this point in this process.

So let's begin...

>> *Breathe in through your nose as you slowly count 1, 2, 3, 4.*

>> *Hold your breath for 1, 2.*

>> *Then, slowly exhale through your mouth 1, 2, 3, 4.*

>> *Repeat until you feel a little calmer and your mind is quieter, or the designated period of time that you chose to meditate for has ended.*

Think about the shift/change you would like to make, and why this is important for you as your life is currently unfolding. Be honest with yourself and remember we are looking to focus on the positive aspect of this shift/change. Now go ahead and write down what you are thinking and feeling.

_____

_____

_____

_____

_____

_____

_____

_____

_____

_____

DAY *6*

You are truly doing an awesome job! There has been a lot going into this foundational shift/change you are making. Take a minute and express how proud you are of your commitment to this process and to YOURSELF!

Today we are going to streamline your shift/change into a positive affirmation. This can be a challenge in and of itself, so hang tight. Look at your shift/change and create a statement that affirms it is already in place. This can be tricky, so let me give you some examples.

EXAMPLE 1:

shift/change: You want to have more free time to spend with friends and family.
Affirmation: I am grateful for the time I spend with friends and family.

EXAMPLE 2:

shift/change: A desire to have financial abundance.
Affirmation: I am blessed to have the means to provide for my needs and wants.

Notice a slight change in the phrasing makes all the difference.

Once you have your positive affirmation, you need to test the statement to see if it is energetically appropriate for you. We might sincerely want to believe in our statement, but our energy needs to resonate with it. If our energy and our statement are not aligned, it will be more of a struggle than it needs to be to create a solid shift/change.

In order to test your statement, you will first need a weighted object. This can be a water bottle, a rock, a book, or anything that has some substance to it, but not too heavy for you to lift with one hand.

Place the object in a location that is level with your arm when it is extended at a 90° angle in front of you. This is generally easier when you are seated. Lift the object up a couple of inches to feel the weight of it. Place the object back down and while in contact with it, say aloud, "My name is _____." When we say a true statement, the object typically feels lighter than the first time we pick it up. Lift it and note the feel of the object.

Repeat the process, this time saying another name that is not your name, nor a nickname of any kind. You should notice when you lift the object while saying the name that is not yours (an untrue statement), the object appears heavier. This will be the same for any untrue statement, being as they are not aligned with your energy. Therefore, if your energy is aligned with your Affirmation Statement, the object you are lifting will most likely feel lighter in comparison to an Affirmation Statement that is not aligned with your energy.

If your statement is not aligned with your energy, you might have to loosen it up a bit. Make it more believable in your mind. The second example stated that there was enough money. But what if you really don't believe that to be true? This is when you would need to play around with the language a bit to find a positive statement that is believable to you. Here are some other options:

> *I am blessed to have the financial means to provide for my needs with money to spare.*
> OR
> *I am grateful to have the financial means to provide for my family's needs.*

Be a little playful with your statements. You want them to make you feel good as you use them. Please don't go too overboard with your wording. We do not want to create any unnecessary stress or anxiety. This would be counterproductive. Tomorrow, you are going to revisit and if needed, refine your Affirmation Statement. So, whether you are in a place where you think you have your statement, or you are starting to feel worked up about it... stop now and meditate.

> » *Breathe in through your nose as you slowly count 1, 2, 3, 4.*
>
> » *Hold your breath for 1, 2.*
>
> » *Then, slowly exhale through your mouth 1, 2, 3, 4.*
>
> » *Repeat until you feel calm and your mind is quiet. You can either let this happen in its natural time, or designate an allotted period of time that you want to meditate for.*

Give yourself some time and acknowledge how well you are doing. Be proud of all of the self-care you are giving yourself by actually taking these action steps for your benefit. You are awesome and totally worth the effort, and the results however they present themselves.

I want to take a moment for clarification regarding manifestation. Although we have certain expectations for the outcome of our shifts/ changes, it is important to not hold onto those too tightly. As humans, we do have a fairly limited perspective of our lives and the possibilities available to us. On the contrary, The Universe has a much broader perspective of how all lives intersect and benefit one another. Add to this their limitless knowledge and it is likely that their vision and expectation for us is far beyond our own imagination.

So, do not get too attached with the exact outcome, instead be open to the possibilities.

DAY 7

It is always a good idea to look at any work in progress with fresh eyes, especially when something is as important as your new Affirmation Statement. So, that is just what we are going to do, after you meditate.

» *Set your intention to open your mind and heart. Take a slow, deep breath in through your nose and release any tension through your mouth in a quick whoosh.*

» *Now, breathe in through your nose as you slowly count 1, 2, 3, 4.*

» *Hold your breath for 1, 2.*

» *Then, slowly exhale through your mouth 1, 2, 3, 4.*

» *Repeat until you feel calm and your mind is quiet.*

Ahhhh.....

Revisit your Affirmation Statement. Do you feel a positivity inside when you say this Affirmation?

Next, test your Affirmation Statement for alignment.

Well, is this the right statement for you? If not, no worries! This is not a tragedy. Inventors almost never perfect their creation on their first, second, or even their third go around. However, they do learn ways to improve on their original ideas. YOU are the inventor of your own reality! So, if you need to go back and create Day 6 - 2.0. Go for it! Just do yourself a favor and take a couple of counting breaths first.

When your Affirmation Statement tests strong and it feels good, then you have the statement that you will enter the next phase of creating your shift/change with.

Congratulations! You are ready to add the next element to your meditation practice. This is a significant step in your journey. Allow yourself to feel both proud and excited.

It is very important to remember not to place any limitations onto our shift/change. Grant The Universe permission to assist you in creating "this", or something better. We never want to limit our possibilities with our own imagination.

As with most subjects, there are a variety of opinions as to how many times one should state their Affirmation. My personal practice is to set aside time in the morning and evening as a part of my meditation. However, I also will say my Affirmation Statement at any point during the day that it comes to mind. As the days go on, the amount of times I say my Affirmation Statement increases.

Remember you tested your Affirmation Statement, so it is important that you say those words. For consistency sake, I recommend having your Affirmation Statement written out. I actually would have several copies on hand and accessible for whenever you may want or need them. This can simply be handwritten on an index card or if you want to get in touch with your creative side/inner child, get crafty! This is not necessary, but it could be fun!

The meditation will include saying your Affirmation Statement seven times. You can use your fingers to keep count, or count beads on a string. I made a simple bracelet for myself. Whichever method of counting you prefer is perfectly fine, as long as it doesn't take you out of your meditation.

Remember, from this point on we are adding the new element to your existing meditation practice.

That being said... let's begin.

AFFIRMATION MEDITATION

» *Set your intention to open your mind and heart. Take a slow, deep breath in through your nose and release any tension through your mouth in a quick whoosh.*

» *Now, breathe in through your nose as you slowly count 1, 2, 3, 4.*

» *Hold your breath for 1, 2.*

» *Then, slowly exhale through your mouth 1, 2, 3, 4.*

» *Repeat until you feel calm and your mind is quiet.*

» *Picture a beautiful ray of sunshine cascading from overhead forming a column of Light all around you.*

» *As you breathe in, pull that Light into your Heart and hold it for as long as it is comfortable, feeling its warmth.*

» *When you exhale, send your Affirmation Statement out to The Universe by saying it aloud. If you can conjure up the feeling of this statement being true, this will add more power to its truth.*

» *Repeat this process seven times.*

Now, take a minute to bask in the feeling of the reality you are creating.

I encourage you to reflect on your meditation experience. This could include how you felt, or thoughts or visions that come to you during your experience. Journaling is great, and another wonderful muscle to exercise as we are gaining more perspective of ourselves and the life we want to create.

DAY *8*

I believe it is important to begin your morning with a meditation to help set the tone for your day. However, if that is not possible for you, meditation can, of course, be practiced at any time.

AFFIRMATION MEDITATION

» *Set your intention to open your mind and heart. Take a slow, deep breath in through your nose and release any tension through your mouth in a quick whoosh.*

» *Now, breathe in through your nose as you slowly count 1, 2, 3, 4.*

» *Hold your breath for 1, 2.*

» *Then, slowly exhale through your mouth 1, 2, 3, 4.*

» *Repeat until you feel calm and your mind is quiet.*

» *Picture a beautiful ray of sunshine cascading from overhead forming a column of Light all around you.*

» *As you breathe in, pull that Light into your Heart and hold it for as long as it is comfortable, feeling its warmth.*

» *When you exhale, send your Affirmation Statement out to The Universe by saying it aloud. Feel the truth of this statement throughout your body.*

» *Repeat this process seven times.*

Now take a minute to bask in the feeling of the reality you are creating. Then journal your thoughts and feelings.

The truth is you already have instances in your life or at some point have experienced the truth of your Affirmation Statement. If you didn't, then you would neither be able to imagine what it would feel like nor would it ever be within your awareness in the first place. It might not be to the level that you are looking to create. Regardless, allow yourself to start finding the evidence of its existence even if you need to look under a microscope!

The more truth you acknowledge in your Affirmation Statement with gratitude, the more you will attract it into your reality. This is why I suggest keeping a written copy of your Affirmation Statement with you at all times. As you see the evidence, state your affirmation loud and proud! Get into the spirit and feel the excitement and gratitude. For example; if your shift/change was about money and you found a penny, be as excited as if you just found $1000! This is an adult version of I Spy... *Affirmation I Spy!*

DAY 9

Now things get a little lighter and more fun! Although the assignments are the same, your experience will be different. The more you acknowledge your experiences with excitement and gratitude, the more profound they will become. Don't rush yourself or The Universe here... that brings in doubt and will have the reverse effect. Seriously, just enjoy the ride!

Remember, you are building your meditation muscle with consistent morning meditations.

AFFIRMATION MEDITATION

» *Set your intention to open your mind and heart. Take a slow, deep breath in through your nose and release any tension through your mouth in a quick whoosh.*

» *Now, breathe in through your nose as you slowly count 1, 2, 3, 4.*

» *Hold your breath for 1, 2.*

» *Then, slowly exhale through your mouth 1, 2, 3, 4.*

» *Repeat until you feel calm and your mind is quiet.*

» *Picture a beautiful ray of sunshine cascading from overhead forming a column of Light all around you.*

» *As you breathe in, pull that Light into your Heart and hold it for as long as it is comfortable, feeling its warmth.*

» *When you exhale, send your Affirmation Statement out to The Universe by saying it aloud. Feel the truth of this statement throughout your body.*

» *Repeat this process 7 times.*

Take a minute to bask in the feeling of the reality you are creating. Then journal your thoughts and feelings.

Great job setting the tone for your day.

Are you ready for a game of *Affirmation I Spy*?

Awesome! Go out and find the evidence of your shift/change that exists in your life right now. Remember, you do not have to do anything different during your day, simply take notice of your evidence with excitement and gratitude! Just as meditation is a muscle to be exercised, so is finding and acknowledging evidence with gratitude.

So, what are you waiting for? Get to it!

DAY *10*

Good morning! Take a nice big stretch and get yourself ready for your mediation.

AFFIRMATION MEDITATION

» *Set your intention to open your mind and heart. Take a slow, deep breath in through your nose and release any tension through your mouth in a quick whoosh.*

» *Now, breathe in through your nose as you slowly count 1, 2, 3, 4.*

» *Hold your breath for 1, 2.*

» *Then, slowly exhale through your mouth 1, 2, 3, 4.*

» *Repeat until you feel calm and your mind is quiet.*

» *Picture a beautiful ray of sunshine cascading from overhead forming a column of Light all around you.*

» *As you breathe in, pull that Light into your Heart and hold it for as long as it is comfortable, feeling its warmth.*

» *When you exhale, send your Affirmation Statement out to The Universe by saying it aloud. Feel the truth of this statement throughout your body.*

» *Repeat this process seven times.*

Take a minute to bask in the feeling of the reality you are creating. Now journal your thoughts and feelings.

_____
_____
_____
_____
_____
_____
_____
_____
_____
_____
_____
_____
_____
_____
_____
_____
_____
_____
_____
_____
_____
_____
_____
_____
_____

Ahhhh, feel the reality that you are creating?

Now you are ready to step into your day and play *Affirmation I Spy!*

DAY *11*

Are you beginning to look forward to your morning meditations?

Do you notice a shift in your reactions to challenging interactions with people, or situations?

This is one of the blessings that mediation brings into our lives. The shifts can overall be huge, but more likely they are subtle as they build. Each person's experience will be unique to them, as are their results both immediate and long term. The one thing that is certain is the stronger your mediation muscle becomes, the greater its positive impact will be on your life as a whole. This is one of the organic shifts I mentioned earlier in this reference book.

So, get yourself situated and begin.

AFFIRMATION MEDITATION

» *Set your intention to open your mind and heart. Take a slow, deep breath in through your nose and release any tension through your mouth in a quick whoosh.*

» *Now, breathe in through your nose as you slowly count 1, 2, 3, 4.*

» *Hold your breath for 1, 2.*

» *Then, slowly exhale through your mouth 1, 2, 3, 4.*

» *Repeat until you feel calm and your mind is quiet.*

» *Picture a beautiful ray of sunshine cascading from overhead forming a column of Light all around you.*

» *As you breathe in, pull that Light into your Heart and hold it for as long as it is comfortable, feeling its warmth.*

» *When you exhale, send your Affirmation Statement out to The Universe by saying it aloud. Feel the truth of this statement throughout your body.*

» *Repeat this process seven times.*

Take a minute to bask in the feeling of the reality you are creating. Now, journal your thoughts and feelings.

As important as it is to recognize the evidence of the of your shifts/ changes in your life, it is equally important that you praise yourself for your effort and commitment to this process. You are gaining strength and courage each day, and reinforcing the understanding that YOU ARE CAPABLE of creating the life you desire and deserve.

Congratulations and keep up the amazing work! I am proud of you. My hope is you are learning to be proud of yourself as well. ♥

You are ready for the next step of this journey. Continue to play Affirmation I Spy throughout your day. Keep feeling excitement and gratitude. Then, take some time at the end of your day to reflect on your evidence. Write them down in statements of Gratitude, including your excitement or other positive feelings regarding the evidence you found. This new layer will keep the evidence you are finding in the forefront of your mind, magnifying the shift you are making. You do not have to write down every single piece of evidence. Choose the ones that bring you the greatest joy!

DAY *12*

It is my hope that as you awaken each morning you are filled with excitement and wonder for what the day holds for you. Consistent morning meditations aid in this positive anticipation of each new day. For the remainder of this 21 day process you will be following the same Affirmation Meditation. However, at the end of this book, I will provide you with an opportunity to acquire other meditations.

AFFIRMATION MEDITATION

» *Set your intention to open your mind and heart. Take a slow, deep breath in through your nose and release any tension through your mouth in a quick whoosh.*

» *Now, breathe in through your nose as you slowly count 1, 2, 3, 4.*

» *Hold your breath for 1, 2.*

» *Then, slowly exhale through your mouth 1, 2, 3, 4.*

» *Repeat until you feel calm and your mind is quiet.*

» *Picture a beautiful ray of sunshine cascading from overhead forming a column of Light all around you.*

» *As you breathe in, pull that Light into your Heart and hold it for as long as it is comfortable, feeling its warmth.*

» *When you exhale, send your Affirmation Statement out to The Universe by saying it aloud. Feel the truth of this statement throughout your body.*

» *Repeat this process seven times.*

Take a minute to bask in the feeling of the reality you are creating. Then journal your thoughts and feelings.

Now, go and enjoy your day, and your game of *Affirmation I Spy!*

Remember to take some time at the end of your day to reflect on your evidence. Write them down in statements of Gratitude, including your excitement or other positive feelings. Choose just a couple of the ones that bring you the greatest joy!

DAY 13

Good morning! Are you ready to start your day? Wonderful, let's begin!

AFFIRMATION MEDITATION

» *Set your intention to open your mind and heart. Take a slow, deep breath in through your nose and release any tension through your mouth in a quick whoosh.*

» *Now, breathe in through your nose as you slowly count 1, 2, 3, 4.*

» *Hold your breath for 1, 2.*

» *Then, slowly exhale through your mouth 1, 2, 3, 4.*

» *Repeat until you feel calm and your mind is quiet.*

» *Picture a beautiful ray of sunshine cascading from overhead.*

» *As you breathe in, fill that light into your Heart and hold.*

» *Feel the warmth, then as your exhale send your Affirmation Statement out to The Universe by stating it aloud. If you can conjure up the feeling of this statement being true all the better!*

» *Repeat seven times.*

Take a minute to bask in the feeling of the reality you are creating. Then journal your thoughts and feelings.

You are doing a fantastic job shifting your energy and mindset. I cannot stress enough how important it is to not only do the work, but have appreciation for YOURSELF and all you are accomplishing. These accomplishments might not be glaring right now, but trust me, if you are following this guide with your complete self, shifts/changes are happening.

Are you ready for your next step?

It is time to look at where your shift/change is being challenged. The reality is that we all face challenges each and every day. Some are small and therefore not as noticeable, while others are wearing a neon sign. What they both have in common is the feeling they elicit.

If the feeling of negativity regarding your shift/change or any other topic creeps up within you, release it and focus on your Affirmative Statement with a positive feeling! Don't judge the negative statement, just refocus.

Please understand you are human, and will experience some sort of negativity in your life. This could emerge from within you, or from another source. Either way try and meet it with the same redirection of focus. Keeping the high vibration of joy and gratitude are key elements in creating your shift/change. Again, feelings are going to come up, however we don't want to stay in that negative energy.

There are going to be times when we cannot redirect our focus to the shift/change we are actively making. The next option I recommend is to turn the situation around. Find the positive aspect or lesson you can take away from this challenging experience. Feel the truth of this turn around within you; feel gratitude.

A good situation to start with is an angry person at the store. The situation might unfold something like this.

Why was that person so nasty? They just walked in front of me and grabbed the last bag of potatoes as if I had done something wrong to them. I can feel their anger. (Deep Breath, Sigh) Maybe they are having a bad day. But, we do not even know each other, how could they be so angry at me? (Slow breath in, slow breath out.) People are often facing challenges others know nothing about, perhaps this is the case here. I am going to let them have some space, and not take this personally. I will walk away as I take some counting breaths. Now that I am calmer, I can honestly wish them peace.

Obviously, turning around a challenging situation isn't always workable. And to be honest, sometimes trying can bring about feelings of frustration, doubt, and unworthiness. This is NOT what you want. Learning when to stop trying to turn things around and shift gears is vital to continuing the forward momentum of bringing your Affirmation Statement to fruition.

Shifting gears is easier when you have a couple of thoughts, memories, visuals at the ready. These are things that when you think of they automatically bring a smile to your face. The best thing is, they don't have to have anything to do with the challenging situation or your Affirmation Statement. They simply need to bring you to a feeling of pure bliss when thought of.

One of my favorites is conjuring up the feeling of walking in the rain on a summer day. The bigger the downpour the more joyful l become. I get giddy and can actually feel the cool water on my skin. I have even caught myself spinning in a circle with my arms outstretched and my face to the sky, while indoors! Yes, I get a questionable look or two from those witnessing my shifting gears, but this just brings me more joy as I hope I lightened their day as well.

When you feel centered again, regardless of which method you use, say your Affirmation Statement with feeling. Repeat it two more times with nice deep breaths between each Affirmation Statement. Then go on with your day in happiness.

Regardless of the twists and turns you experienced, remember at the end of your day to take some time to reflect on the evidence of your shift/change occurring. Write them down in statements of Gratitude, including your joy or other positive feelings, will magnify the shift/ change you are making.

_____
_____
_____
_____
_____
_____
_____
_____
_____
_____
_____
_____
_____
_____
_____
_____
_____
_____
_____
_____
_____
_____
_____
_____
_____
_____
_____

DAY *14*

Congratulations! You are more than halfway through this process. It has taken diligence as well as an open mind and heart to come this far. Give yourself a hug from me, I think you are doing great!

This is the perfect opportunity to remind you to stay in the moment as you continue on your journey. At this point in this process you will be doing the exact same meditations as well as responding to the same journal prompts. I know this may feel redundant. I understand that repetition can cause some people to diminish the value of their efforts. I also know how incredibly important it is to ingrain this process into your muscle memory!

You are doing two strength training exercises through this process, the first is building your meditation muscle. We have already touched on the importance meditation has in bringing a calming shift in how we handle difficult situations.

The second strength training exercise is the muscle memory that is being established to see the evidence supporting your Affirmation Statement. Being able to spot this evidence with consistency is the first phase of manifesting. The second phase is believing in its truth. This is when the real magic begins to happen. Now you are tipping the scales to truly AFFIRMING THE REALITY YOU ARE CREATING. The more natural it becomes to find the evidence of your desires, the quicker and easier it is to manifest anything. This is when things really get fun!

I implore you to allow yourself to flow through this process until it becomes second nature. In order to make the rest of this process as seamless as possible for you, it will simply be copy and pasted with only the number of the day you are on changing. Continue moving page by page immersing yourself into the experiences of meditation, journaling and playing *Affirmation I Spy*.

AFFIRMATION MEDITATION

» *Set your intention to open your mind and heart. Take a slow, deep breath in through your nose and release any tension through your mouth in a quick whoosh.*

» *Now, breathe in through your nose as you slowly count 1, 2, 3, 4.*

» *Hold your breath for 1, 2.*

» *Then, slowly exhale through your mouth 1, 2, 3, 4.*

» *Repeat until you feel calm and your mind is quiet.*

» *Picture a beautiful ray of sunshine cascading from overhead forming a column of Light all around you.*

» *As you breathe in, pull that Light into your Heart and hold it for as long as it is comfortable, feeling its warmth.*

» *When you exhale, send your Affirmation Statement out to The Universe by saying it aloud. Feel the truth of this statement throughout your body.*

» *Repeat this process seven times.*

Take a minute to bask in the feeling of the reality you are creating. Then journal your thoughts and feelings.

_____

_____

_____

_____

_____

_____

_____

_____

_____

_____

_____

_____

_____

_____

_____

_____

_____

_____

_____

_____

_____

_____

_____

_____

Now, go and enjoy your day, and your game of *Affirmation I Spy!*

Remember to take some time at the end of your day to reflect on your evidence. Write them down in statements of Gratitude, including your excitement or other positive feelings. Choose just a couple of the ones that bring you the greatest joy!

DAY *15*

AFFIRMATION MEDITATION

» *Set your intention to open your mind and heart. Take a slow, deep breath in through your nose and release any tension through your mouth in a quick whoosh.*

» *Now, breathe in through your nose as you slowly count 1, 2, 3, 4.*

» *Hold your breath for 1, 2.*

» *Then, slowly exhale through your mouth 1, 2, 3, 4.*

» *Repeat until you feel calm and your mind is quiet.*

» *Picture a beautiful ray of sunshine cascading from overhead forming a column of Light all around you.*

» *As you breathe in, pull that Light into your Heart and hold it for as long as it is comfortable, feeling its warmth.*

» *When you exhale, send your Affirmation Statement out to The Universe by saying it aloud. Feel the truth of this statement throughout your body.*

» *Repeat this process seven times.*

Take a minute to bask in the feeling of the reality you are creating. Then journal your thoughts and feelings.

_____

_____

_____

_____

_____

_____

_____

_____

_____

_____

_____

_____

_____

_____

_____

_____

_____

_____

_____

_____

_____

_____

_____

_____

_____

Now, go and enjoy your day, and your game of *Affirmation I Spy!*

Remember to take some time at the end of your day to reflect on your evidence. Write them down in statements of Gratitude, including your excitement or other positive feelings. Choose just a couple of the ones that bring you the greatest joy!

DAY *16*

AFFIRMATION MEDITATION

» *Set your intention to open your mind and heart. Take a slow, deep breath in through your nose and release any tension through your mouth in a quick whoosh.*

» *Now, breathe in through your nose as you slowly count 1, 2, 3, 4.*

» *Hold your breath for 1, 2.*

» *Then, slowly exhale through your mouth 1, 2, 3, 4.*

» *Repeat until you feel calm and your mind is quiet.*

» *Picture a beautiful ray of sunshine cascading from overhead forming a column of Light all around you.*

» *As you breathe in, pull that Light into your Heart and hold it for as long as it is comfortable, feeling its warmth.*

» *When you exhale, send your Affirmation Statement out to The Universe by saying it aloud. Feel the truth of this statement throughout your body.*

» *Repeat this process seven times.*

Take a minute to bask in the feeling of the reality you are creating. Then journal your thoughts and feelings.

_____

_____

_____

_____

_____

_____

_____

_____

_____

_____

_____

_____

_____

_____

_____

_____

_____

_____

_____

_____

_____

_____

_____

_____

_____

_____

Now, go and enjoy your day, and your game of *Affirmation I Spy!*

Remember to take some time at the end of your day to reflect on your evidence. Write them down in statements of Gratitude, including your excitement or other positive feelings. Choose just a couple of the ones that bring you the greatest joy!

DAY *17*

AFFIRMATION MEDITATION

» *Set your intention to open your mind and heart. Take a slow, deep breath in through your nose and release any tension through your mouth in a quick whoosh.*

» *Now, breathe in through your nose as you slowly count 1, 2, 3, 4.*

» *Hold your breath for 1, 2.*

» *Then, slowly exhale through your mouth 1, 2, 3, 4.*

» *Repeat until you feel calm and your mind is quiet.*

» *Picture a beautiful ray of sunshine cascading from overhead forming a column of Light all around you.*

» *As you breathe in, pull that Light into your Heart and hold it for as long as it is comfortable, feeling its warmth.*

» *When you exhale, send your Affirmation Statement out to The Universe by saying it aloud. Feel the truth of this statement throughout your body.*

» *Repeat this process seven times.*

Take a minute to bask in the feeling of the reality you are creating. Then journal your thoughts and feelings.

_____
_____
_____
_____
_____
_____
_____
_____
_____
_____
_____
_____
_____
_____
_____
_____
_____
_____
_____
_____
_____
_____
_____
_____
_____
_____

Now, go and enjoy your day, and your game of *Affirmation I Spy!*

Remember to take some time at the end of your day to reflect on your evidence. Write them down in statements of Gratitude, including your excitement or other positive feelings. Choose just a couple of the ones that bring you the greatest joy!

DAY *18*

AFFIRMATION MEDITATION

» *your intention to open your mind and heart. Take a slow, deep breath in through your nose and release any tension through your mouth in a quick whoosh.*

» *Now, breathe in through your nose as you slowly count 1, 2, 3, 4.*

» *Hold your breath for 1, 2.*

» *Then, slowly exhale through your mouth 1, 2, 3, 4.*

» *Repeat until you feel calm and your mind is quiet.*

» *Picture a beautiful ray of sunshine cascading from overhead forming a column of Light all around you.*

» *As you breathe in, pull that Light into your Heart and hold it for as long as it is comfortable, feeling its warmth.*

» *When you exhale, send your Affirmation Statement out to The Universe by saying it aloud. Feel the truth of this statement throughout your body.*

» *Repeat this process seven times.*

Take a minute to bask in the feeling of the reality you are creating. Then journal your thoughts and feelings.

_____

_____

_____

_____

_____

_____

_____

_____

_____

_____

_____

_____

_____

_____

_____

_____

_____

_____

_____

_____

_____

_____

_____

_____

_____

_____

Now, go and enjoy your day, and your game of *Affirmation I Spy!*

Remember to take some time at the end of your day to reflect on your evidence. Write them down in statements of Gratitude, including your excitement or other positive feelings. Choose just a couple of the ones that bring you the greatest joy!

DAY *19*

AFFIRMATION MEDITATION

» *Set your intention to open your mind and heart. Take a slow, deep breath in through your nose and release any tension through your mouth in a quick whoosh.*

» *Now, breathe in through your nose as you slowly count 1, 2, 3, 4.*

» *Hold your breath for 1, 2.*

» *Then, slowly exhale through your mouth 1, 2, 3, 4.*

» *Repeat until you feel calm and your mind is quiet.*

» *Picture a beautiful ray of sunshine cascading from overhead forming a column of Light all around you.*

» *As you breathe in, pull that Light into your Heart and hold it for as long as it is comfortable, feeling its warmth.*

» *When you exhale, send your Affirmation Statement out to The Universe by saying it aloud. Feel the truth of this statement throughout your body.*

» *Repeat this process seven times.*

Take a minute to bask in the feeling of the reality you are creating. Then journal your thoughts and feelings.

_____

_____

_____

_____

_____

_____

_____

_____

_____

_____

_____

_____

_____

_____

_____

_____

_____

_____

_____

_____

_____

_____

_____

_____

_____

_____

Now, go and enjoy your day, and your game of *Affirmation I Spy!*

Remember to take some time at the end of your day to reflect on your evidence. Write them down in statements of Gratitude, including your excitement or other positive feelings. Choose just a couple of the ones that bring you the greatest joy!

DAY *20*

AFFIRMATION MEDITATION

» *Set your intention to open your mind and heart. Take a slow, deep breath in through your nose and release any tension through your mouth in a quick whoosh.*

» *Now, breathe in through your nose as you slowly count 1, 2, 3, 4.*

» *Hold your breath for 1, 2.*

» *Then, slowly exhale through your mouth 1, 2, 3, 4.*

» *Repeat until you feel calm and your mind is quiet.*

» *Picture a beautiful ray of sunshine cascading from overhead forming a column of Light all around you.*

» *As you breathe in, pull that Light into your Heart and hold it for as long as it is comfortable, feeling its warmth.*

» *When you exhale, send your Affirmation Statement out to The Universe by saying it aloud. Feel the truth of this statement throughout your body.*

» *Repeat this process seven times.*

Take a minute to bask in the feeling of the reality you are creating. Then journal your thoughts and feelings.

_____

_____

_____

_____

_____

_____

_____

_____

_____

_____

_____

_____

_____

_____

_____

_____

_____

_____

_____

_____

_____

_____

_____

Now, go and enjoy your day, and your game of *Affirmation I Spy!*

Remember to take some time at the end of your day to reflect on your evidence. Write them down in statements of Gratitude, including your excitement or other positive feelings. Choose just a couple of the ones that bring you the greatest joy!

DAY *21*

AFFIRMATION MEDITATION

» *Set your intention to open your mind and heart. Take a slow, deep breath in through your nose and release any tension through your mouth in a quick whoosh.*

» *Now, breathe in through your nose as you slowly count 1, 2, 3, 4.*

» *Hold your breath for 1, 2.*

» *Then, slowly exhale through your mouth 1, 2, 3, 4.*

» *Repeat until you feel calm and your mind is quiet.*

» *Picture a beautiful ray of sunshine cascading from overhead forming a column of Light all around you.*

» *As you breathe in, pull that Light into your Heart and hold it for as long as it is comfortable, feeling its warmth.*

» *When you exhale, send your Affirmation Statement out to The Universe by saying it aloud. Feel the truth of this statement throughout your body.*

» *Repeat this process seven times.*

Take a minute to bask in the feeling of the reality you are creating. Then journal your thoughts and feelings.

_____

_____

_____

_____

_____

_____

_____

_____

_____

_____

_____

_____

_____

_____

_____

_____

_____

_____

_____

_____

_____

_____

_____

_____

_____

_____

_____

Now, go and enjoy your day, and your game of *Affirmation I Spy!*

Remember to take some time at the end of your day to reflect on your evidence. Write them down in statements of Gratitude, including your excitement or other positive feelings. Choose just a couple of the ones that bring you the greatest joy!

Congratulations! You did it!!! I am hoping you have at least as much pride in yourself for completing this process as I did in creating it. This was no small feat. You should be congratulated for not only completing the process, but for knowing you were worthy of doing so. Hats off to you!

Now, everyone's personal amount of shift/change will vary based on their individual circumstances. This includes, but is not limited to their consistency, the shift/change they chose, how the chosen shift/change is related to their life lesson, and where they are on their Spiritual Journey. None of this is a judgment in any way, it is more factual.

If you want to see more of a shift/change with this Affirmation Statement in your reality, do the process again. Often, we do need to go through it more than once. Each time our Affirmation Statement should be altered to reflect the shifts we have made. Remember at the beginning of the process we had to align with our Affirmation Statement. Some shifts were too big at the time and needed to be made more believable for us. This would be your opportunity to reach further into the shift you are truly wanting to make possible.

Or maybe your vision for your life has altered due to the experience you have had with the process. That is awesome, too! Create an entirely new Affirmation Statement and work through the process in a whole new light.

This was never meant to be a one and done process. Use it again and again! There is no limit to how this relatively simple process can assist you in reaching goals, and finding peace and happiness.

I promised you earlier access to other guided meditations to expand your personal practice.

You can find these on my YouTube channel youtube.com/@DrStaciSnair.

You can also access this and other offerings on my website
http://www.drstacisnair.com

Wishing you many blessings.

With much Love,
Dr. Staci

ABOUT THE AUTHOR

As a young child, I always knew there was so much more to our world than our eyes could see. I was sheltered, and experienced a very traditional upbringing. Yet, I still held onto this unexplainable knowing that our world was a mere piece of a much, much larger puzzle.

Later in life tragedy would confirm what I had always known to be my truth. In the year 2001, my son, Ethan, suddenly left our world. I was devastated, but again my intuition told me this was for a reason. This intuition guided me to study myself and the workings of our Universe. I learned to be still and listen to the guidance around me. Before long something inside me changed, and an inner peace that I never knew existed filled my heart. Over time a series of synchronistic events led me to broaden my skill set so that I could share what I have learned with others. I now know that the purpose of Ethan's leaving our physical world was to wake me up to what was inside me all along.

My healing also became my mission, to share the tools and wisdom I have learned with others. I have offered many services and classes through the years, and now I share this beautiful book. My intention is to ignite a spark of Hope that we are all capable of achieving Healing and Peace in our own lives.

www.ingramcontent.com/pod-product-compliance
Lightning Source LLC
Chambersburg PA
CBHW070934120626
46546CB00004B/1412